3 a.m. notes

Eileen Veatch

Presentation by *BookLeaf Publishing*

Web: www.bookleafpub.com

E-mail: info@bookleafpub.com

ISBN: 9789358367676

First edition 2023

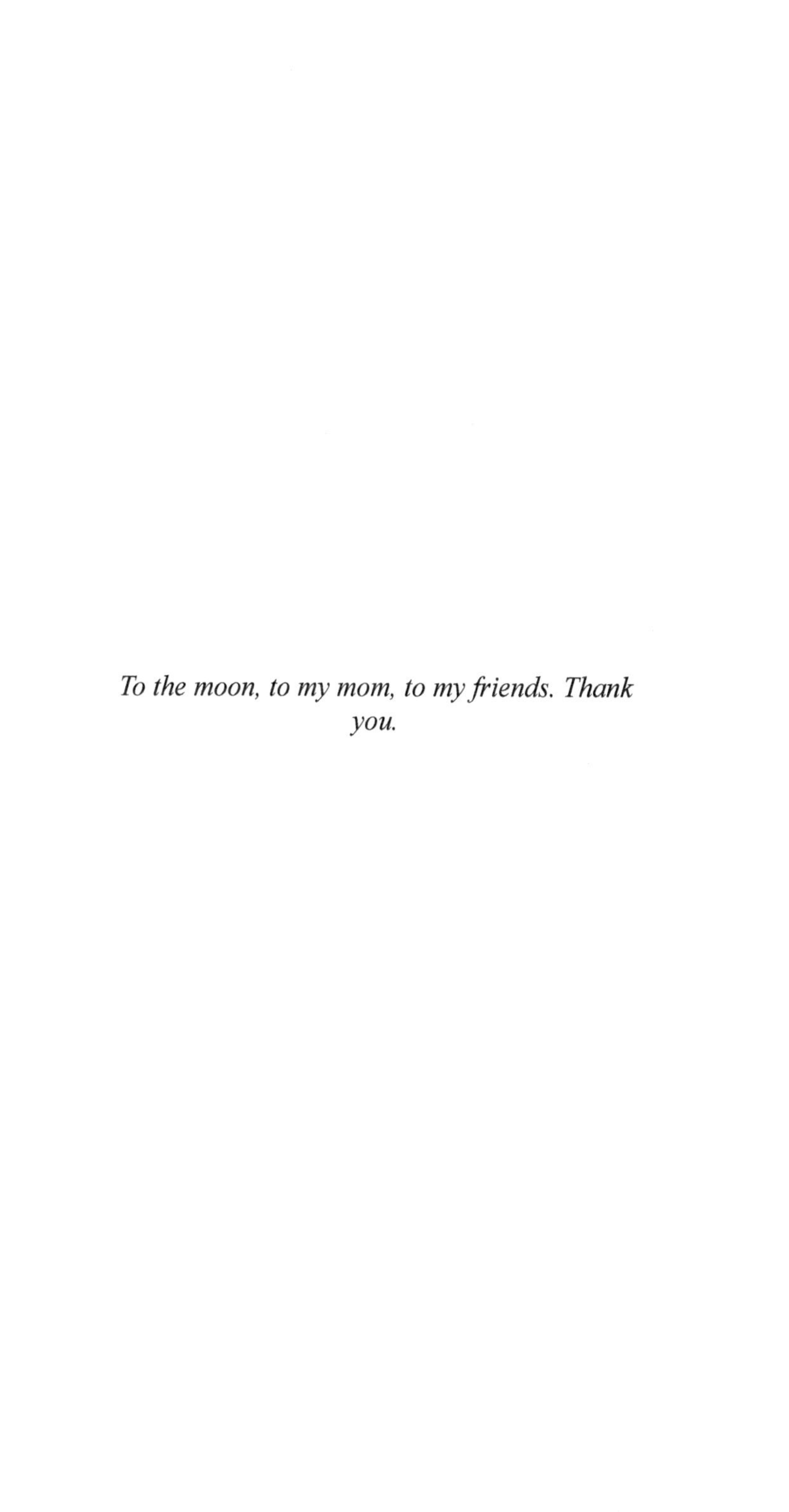

To the moon, to my mom, to my friends. Thank you.

Sprinkles

I hate sprinkles.
Do you know how much of a buzzkill
you have to be to say that you hate sprinkles?

I mean come on!
They're tiny capsules of sugar!
Happiness!
But god, I hate sprinkles.

I hate the way they taste.
Kind of like chemicals.
Kind of like nothing.
They always ruin the cupcake.

And don't get me started on the colors.
The bright, vibrant colors pulling you in
Exciting you like a smile on a mask
That hides the bitterness underneath.

You want to know the worst part?

I hate their size.
Their tiny, skinny size.
Full of sugar,
Mocking me.

I hate sprinkles because
I hate that they mock me.
I hate that they are everything
I can't seem to be.

Because everyone looks at sprinkles
And their faces light up.
I look at sprinkles,
And I get jealous.

I hate sprinkles because
I hate that they can mask
Themselves into something
Everybody seems to love.

I hate sprinkles because
I hate the way I am.

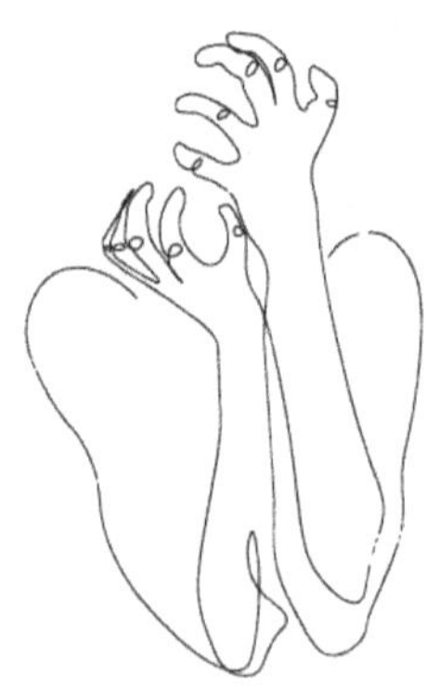

Bound (Haunted)

The ghosts, they lay
In my hand.
Following like shadows
On command.

As close as space.
As far as skin.
Where I end and where
They begin.

Suffocate the
Body, they hound.
I beg the ghosts to
Leave me un-

Lists

My Fridays tend to go something like this:
One.
I wake up at 6 am and remember that it's Friday while I get ready for school. It's only been four days since Sunday, but I can't wait for the weekend.
Two.
I get to school and I go through the same classes I always do. I talk to my friends and I go to lunch and I talk some more. I smile and laugh and talk about how ready I am for the weekend.
Three.
The bell finally rings and I stand in the hallway with my friends waiting for the parking lot to clear. And I'm so tired. So exhausted. I can't wait to go home for the weekend.
Four.
I throw my book bag in the corner, and I fall onto my bed. I have the whole weekend for nothing.
Five.
I scroll my phone for a bit and decide a quick nap wouldn't hurt.
Six.

I wake up at six when my mom calls for dinner.
I didn't mean to sleep that long. How could I
waste three hours of my weekend?
Seven.
It's ten now and I made my lights blue. I have
my favorite show on the tv, but it's paused so I
can scroll my phone some more.
Eight.
Scrolling social media turns to scrolling through
pictures and memories. God I miss when I felt
like that. Now I'm just tired and bored all the
time. I do the same thing every week.
Nine.
It's midnight now and I'm tired but if I go to
bed, I have to start a new day the next morning
and I don't want to do that yet. The only time
that I feel myself is when no one else is awake. I
have all this time to think and think. And
thinking turns to panic and I add to my list of
things I'm worried about. I like lists. I thought
keeping a list would make me feel better but
when I reread it I can't breath and my head hurts
and my gut squeezes and
Ten.
Nine. Eight. Seven. Six. Five. Four. Three. Two.
One.
I hit my thumb against the pad of each finger
forward and backward forward and backward
forward and-

I lay on my cold floor and text my best friend.
But it's three in the morning now and all my
friends are asleep and I'm alone with my
thoughts and they get so scary so fast and- why
do I do that?
God why can't I be normal? I could go to sleep
now. I could stop this panic and begin a new day.
But this is how every Friday goes and who am I
if I'm not the same pattern every week? I find
comfort in my pain. Regularity. Like a list.

Day One

Today on my way home
I saw my first butterfly
In few months.
It made me smile.

And as I continued driving,
I saw that the fields that surrounded
Me were greener than they'd
Been yesterday.

When I let my dogs outside,
My cat had followed onto the porch
And I watched his head whip around
Watching the flies outside.

I walked into my room
And even though it was already
Stifling with the heat from outside,
I opened the curtains.

I sat on my bed and thought
About that butterfly.
I think it was orange but
I had been too distracted to tell for sure.

But regardless I wanted
To remember how happy it made me
So I grabbed pen and paper
And wrote how…

Friendship Breakup

Missing someone who isn't gone hurts so bad.
I still know where you live
I still remember your favorite color
I still remember the music you listen to
I still remember the way you dance
I still know your favorite animal
I still laugh at the jokes
I still see you in everything.

You're right there.

I miss who I used to be around you.
I want to tell you everything,
But I don't want to bother you.
I miss you so much.
But we don't talk anymore.

Please Forgive Me

Your body is a temple,
Gods and goddesses divine.
But they sit with their rib cages showing
Because sometimes I refuse
To feed my body.

Your body is a temple,
Gods and goddesses divine.
And scars mark their skin
Because sometimes when I feel
Too much my nails leave trails.

Gods and goddesses divine,
I ask for your forgiveness because
I promise I'm trying to get better.
I'm trying to shelter you
In my temple of a body.

You see, because sometimes
I don't feel like leaving the bed.
And sometimes I don't feel like
This temple is good enough.
Yet you still stay.

I tear you down and you string
Lights across my heart.

Unrequited

I think I could love the moon,
If she loved me back.

But she only talks
Among the stars.
Telling the jokes
That once were ours.

Stage 1

I found myself looking at her again.

I keep telling myself,
"It's only because I want to look like her."
But I know it's more than that.
Because I find myself doodling my favorite parts
of her during my math class.

The curve of her shoulder.
The slope of her neck.
Her lips.
Her eyes.
Her.

Her ivory skin.
Her oversized jacket.
And I know whether she kept her light hair or
changed it to dark again,
I'd feel the same.

It's her.

Night 129

I want to push my hand in my stomach,
Reach up past my rib cage,
Pull my heart out,
And throw it on the ground.

God.

I'd rather walk miles on broken glass
Than face what you left for me.
Countless nights of tears
Yet defending you to my friends.

And you won't ever get that.
Cause you would still make it
Feel like it's my fault
That I was always there for you.

"I don't want to live in a hole anymore"

Some people are scared of spiders
Snakes
The dark
Being alone
Heights
Rejection.
I'm scared of 9-5 office jobs.

The moon is beautiful, isn't it?

You began using that line
After our first fight.
I'm not sure what made you
Start saying it then.

You had known how much
I loved the moon.
I suppose maybe you
Were trying to connect with me.

But I don't think you realize what you've done.

Because I used to look into
The sky every night.
And no matter what phase it was,
I'd look for the moon.

And you knew that.
Sometimes when I didn't feel
Like leaving the bed,
You would remind me so I would get up.

But then you started
Texting that stupid line.

A beautiful line.
Your only line.

Because eventually all
Your "sorry" texts meant nothing.
And that stupid line would
Light up my screen.

You used my one thing against me.

Did you know I've stopped looking for the
moon in the sky?

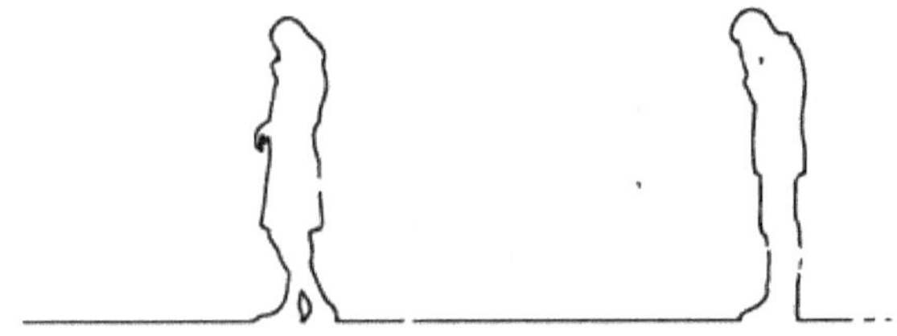

People Pleaser

I tell them it's alright.
No really, I'm fine.
And no matter how I try,
I can't draw a line.

They're pushing my boundaries.
My limbs keep stretching.
They come with their knives,
And leave more etchings.

I gave him my food.
I gave her my water.
If I give it first,
It isn't slaughter.

I've given all I have.
They take my flowers.
And when I cry,
It gives them showers.

What you left me

I want to go to a place no one has ever been
before.
I want to lay on the cold floor of dirt and moss
and grass and bugs and I want to seep deep into
every pore.
I want to adore everything that you abhor.

In fact, I want to be everything that you abhor.
And when you see the debris from the war you'll
scream your plea and I want to be there.

I'm already covered in your scars and no plea to
Mars will save you from the bars you built.

You will never be my light again.

Picture this.
There is a moth flying around a room.
Not just any room, but a room with no windows.
No light.
That's me.
Now picture this.
There is now a candle in the room.
A candle bright enough to light the corners.
That's you.
Now, stay with me and picture this.
I am still bouncing off the walls,
Searching for the light.
Even though it's right there!
Even as I fly over you and feel your warmth,
I don't recognize you as light.
Silly moth.
Don't you need the light?
Don't you want the light?
The truth is, I do.
But I keep my eyes closed as I fly around the
room
Looking for a place you haven't touched.
Because even though I need the light,
I don't want to be burned.

I would rather fly into wall after wall
Until I can finally break free
Before I ever come close to you again.
Because I don't even recognize you as light
anymore.

Perspective

Sometimes I wish I could live life without my
glasses.
That way I wouldn't be able to read the news
being spread to the masses.
So I could blur the body that appears in the
mirror.
Or the acne that scars my face when I step
nearer.

But then how would I see the way my best
friend's smile lights the room.
Or when spring comes, and my favorite flowers
start to bloom.
How would I see when the rain follows the
thunderstorms like twins,

Or admire the freckles on that one girl's
champagne skin.
How could I read the words my favorite authors
write,
Or the way the moon lights up the night.

Even though not everything is nice to see,
I'd say the little things make up plenty.

A love poem

I love your eyes.
I love your hair.
Sometimes I love your skin.
I love your touch.
I love your smile.
Sometimes I love your feelings.
I love your shoulders.
I love your passion.
I really love your imagination.

- From me to me

Selfish

I sat in front of my phone waiting to break up
with you.
I told you I needed a break, and we stopped
talking for a week.
Only one week, but I have never felt so much
relief.
I hung out with my friends, and I didn't need to
babysit your tantrums.
And if you ever read this, you would shut me out
forever.
Or maybe you would text me sorry again like the
five million other times.
And when you called, I had my speech planned
out.
But then you brought up the same old thing.
The thing that we have already talked about!
It was like déjà vu repeating that same
conversation.
"Sorry."
"It's fine."
I don't even know what you were apologizing
for.
I don't even know if you know either.
I don't even care anymore.
You're about to hang up.

"Anything else?"
I am giving you the opportunity to ask. Or
maybe break it off first. Because I think you
already know my answer and you're scared.
"Nope."
And we hang up.
And my heart rate slows down.
Maybe I'm scared too. Of what you'll do.
Not to me, believe me I know you never want to
hurt me.
But of what you'll do to yourself.
Because you don't know that what you are doing
to yourself scares me more than anything you
could ever do to me.

A note for future me

Please never stop jumping up and down when you get excited.
Please never stop playing music louder than you can sing in the car.
Please never stop saying "cows!" or "horsies!" when you see them.
Please never stop having concerts in front of the mirror or in the shower.
Please never stop giggling at inappropriate jokes.
Please never stop getting excited over new bookmarks.
Please never stop telling mom every tiny thing.

Please never stop dancing around your room to Taylor Swift.
Please never stop screaming over books.
Please never stop drawing suns on the corner of the paper.
Please never stop calling dogs "puppies" no matter how old they are.
Please never stop being yourself.
Please never lose yourself.
I don't want to lose myself.

She was there.

She was there that night we got ice cream and you asked me to be your girlfriend.
She was there the nights before that when we would lay on the hammock and point at the stars.
She was there tonight, as we met in the park and you ended things.
She was there the nights I spent crying over you and the things you did.
And she was even there the nights I didn't look for her.
So tonight, I turn to the moon.
I don't need to apologize. She knows.
I don't need to explain that it's still hard to look at her because when I do, I reminds me of him.
She understands.
So tonight, as I stand on my porch, we look back at each other in silence.
We know. We understand.